NOSES

Santa Fe Writers Group

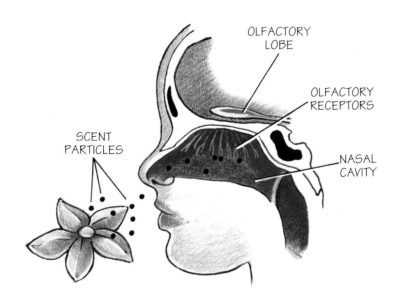

OLFACTORY
LOBE

OLFACTORY
RECEPTORS

NASAL
CAVITY

SCENT
PARTICLES

**John Muir Publications
Santa Fe, New Mexico**

Special thanks to Mary Colleen McNamara, Ph.D., Department of Biology, Albuquerque Technical-Vocational Institute, Albuquerque, New Mexico

Santa Fe Writers Group:
Richard Harris, research
K. C. Compton
Donald E. Fineberg
Kathleen Lee
Miriam Sagan
Leda Silver

John Muir Publications, P.O. Box 613, Santa Fe, New Mexico 87504

First edition. First printing September 1993
First TWG printing September 1993

Library of Congress Cataloging-in-Publication Data
Bizarre & beautiful noses / Santa Fe Writers Group.
    p. cm.
    Includes index.
    Summary: Describes the noses and sense of smell of such diverse animals as the lemur, turkey vulture, and salmon.
    ISBN 1-56261-124-0 : $14.95
    1. Smell—Juvenile literature. 2. Nose—Juvenile literature. 3. Physiology, Comparative—Juvenile literature. 4. Animals—Physiology—Juvenile literature.
[1. Smell. 2. Senses and sensation. 3. Nose. 4. Animals—Physiology.] I. Santa Fe Writers Group. II. Title: Bizarre and beautiful noses.
QP458.B57 1993
591.1'826—dc20
                                                                93-19593
                                                                    CIP
                                                                    AC

Logo/Interior design: Ken Wilson   591.1
Illustrations: Chris Brigman   B
Typography: Ken Wilson
Printer: Guynes Printing Company

Distributed to the book trade by
W. W. Norton & Co., Inc.
500 Fifth Ave.
New York, New York 10110

Distributed to the education market by
The Wright Group
19201 120th Avenue NE
Bothell, WA 98011

Cover photo, spatulate nose treefrog, Animals Animals © Zig Leszczynski
Back cover photo, Gothic bat, Animals Animals © Michael Fogden

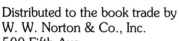
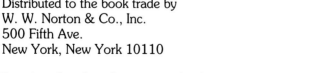

INtroduction

All animals on the planet, including humans, understand the world around them by using sensory organs. The senses we know the most about are sight, smell, taste, touch, and hearing. Animals use these senses to avoid predators, to find mates, food, and shelter, and to entertain themselves. Some people believe that animals, including humans, use other, less-understood senses as well. Have you ever had a "hunch" about something that proved to be true? Maybe you were using a sense other than one of the five mentioned above.

The sense of smell, also called **olfaction**, serves many purposes. The female moth releases a potent perfume to attract the male moth. Honeybees follow a scent trail of nectar or pollen to the flower that promises a harvest. And many animals track their prey by the trail of scent it leaves behind.

Bizarre & Beautiful Noses investigates the sense of smell in the animal kingdom. But before we meet the twenty animals featured in this book, let's go over the basics of smell.

Dogs have one of the keenest senses of smell.

Honeybees smell with the hair-like sensilla on their antennae.

Honeybee

LED BY THE NOSE

The sense of smell is especially important in detecting danger, even for humans. We can smell a fire, for example, even when we cannot see or hear it. The advance warning gives us a better chance of escaping the danger. Our sense of smell also unlocks the world of pleasant fragrances—our favorite foods cooking, the outdoors, flowers in bloom, or the salty spray of the ocean. And if we couldn't smell, much of our food would be tasteless to us.

Our sense of smell can warn us of danger. It also allows us to enjoy pleasant fragrances.

Different animals tune in to different odors and ignore or avoid others. For example, a cat will probably turn its nose up at your vegetable garden, but a rabbit will show great interest in the fragrance of carrots and lettuce. This is because animals pay attention to the smells that are important to their survival. Humans can identify thousands of odors, but smell is not one of our most important senses.

What Smells?

Daisies smell fresh, pineapples smell fruity, attics smell musty, and dogs . . . just plain smell! But no matter how we might describe them, all odors are tiny particles of chemical substances that are carried through air, water, or earth and are detected by animals' smelling organs.

Most species of animals have a distinct odor. For example, even with your eyes closed and your ears plugged, you could still probably tell the difference between a parrot and a horse by the way each smells. Animals smell a certain way because of what they eat, where they live, and the natural scents they produce. Many animals have scent glands that secrete a substance that other members of their species can detect. This chemical substance is called a **pheromone** (FAIR-uh-moan). Humans as a species also have a distinct scent (just ask any deer during hunting season). Each individual person, too, has a unique smell. This scent is most likely pleasant to the people who care about us and may be unpleasant to people who dislike us. Think about it: Do you tend to like the smell of people you care about? Do you associate certain smells with certain feelings, activities, or people? It's no surprise if you do: in most people, smells trigger memories more than any other sense.

Smells trigger memories more than any other sense.

Olfactory Organs

Not all smelling organs are conventional noses, snouts, or beaks. The elephant's long trunk, for example, is a multipurpose organ the animal uses to breathe, smell, spray water, feed itself, move obstacles out of the way, and even hug its children. The snake has two openings in the roof of the mouth called the Jacobson's organ with which it smells. A mosquito's smelling organs are on its antennae, as are the

SAVORY SMELLS

When you have a cold and your nose is stuffy, you can't smell a thing. And no wonder: your nasal passages are swollen from inflammation (painful irritation of tissue). This swelling prevents scent molecules from reaching the olfactory receptors far up in your nasal cavities. You may also have noticed that foods you normally love taste bland and boring when you're stuffed up. This is because the sense of smell is all wrapped up with the sense of taste. Flavors are detected by the taste buds covering our tongues, but our perception of them is strengthened by the odors that tag along. These odors travel to the olfactory receptors through your throat as well as through your nose. This is why professional wine tasters swirl the glass of wine under their nose before taking a sip. They are releasing scent molecules from the liquid so they can "taste" the smell of the wine as well as its flavor. Next time you have a cold, close your eyes and put a slice of apple on your tongue and then a slice of raw potato. Can you tell the difference between them?

The sense of smell is directly linked to the sense of taste. That's why food tastes bland when you have a cold.

bee's and moth's. And some species of salamander breathe and smell right through their skin!

Sensing Scents

But whatever the type of organ, all smell is possible because of cells called **olfactory receptors**. Throughout the animal kingdom, these are simple nerve cells with hair-like projections to receive scent molecules. Some animals have greater numbers of olfactory receptors than others, and the receptors are not on the same part of each animal's body. But the way in which the receptors are activated and pass their information on to the brain is the same across species.

The chemical particles that make up odors must first be dissolved before they can be smelled. When the chemicals reach the olfactory receptors, they are turned into signals to be sent to the **olfactory lobe**, the part of the brain that interprets smell. The brain determines what the smell is and then tells the animal what action to take, if any.

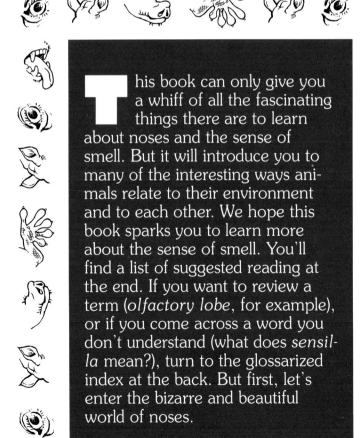

This book can only give you a whiff of all the fascinating things there are to learn about noses and the sense of smell. But it will introduce you to many of the interesting ways animals relate to their environment and to each other. We hope this book sparks you to learn more about the sense of smell. You'll find a list of suggested reading at the end. If you want to review a term (*olfactory lobe*, for example), or if you come across a word you don't understand (what does *sensilla* mean?), turn to the glossarized index at the back. But first, let's enter the bizarre and beautiful world of noses.

Mosquitoes

(Genus: *Culex*)

osquitoes don't have noses like ours, but they can still smell. The very fine sensory hairs on their long antennae detect both odors and temperature. Have you ever wondered why mosquitoes seem especially fond of buzzing around your head? It's because you, like all mammals, exhale carbon dioxide. The mosquito's antennae search for carbon dioxide and changes in air temperature because both are clues that a warm-blooded animal is nearby—and that means a meal. Both male and female mosquitoes drink nectar from flowers, but only female mosquitoes drink blood. This is because most types of mosquitoes need a blood meal to develop their eggs.

Mosquitoes are among the most dangerous insects to human beings because many species carry serious diseases. That's why people have invented ways to repel mosquitoes, such as window screens, net drapes over beds, and chemical sprays. If a mosquito flying toward a meal smells something unpleasant, such as a chemical repellent, it changes course and heads in the other direction. Fortunately, you don't have to drench yourself with repellent to keep mosquitoes from pestering you. Usually, it's enough to cover your socks or some other part of your clothing, or even the floor of a porch. Mosquitoes are bothered by the smell of the repellent in the air, not on your skin.

Mosquitoes also use their sense of smell to find a place to nest. They need to lay their eggs in very still ponds or puddles. The insects are attracted to stagnant water by the sweet smell of bacteria that grow in it.

REPEL THE NATURAL WAY

Some unfortunate people are very attractive to mosquitoes. Others, for some mysterious reason, are never bothered by them. Scientists suspect the difference has something to do with the chemicals in human sweat. Fortunately, there are other natural odors that turn mosquitoes off: pennyroyal, eucalyptus, citronella, lavender, and cinnamon are some of them. Some campers rub these oils on their clothing to ward off the pests.

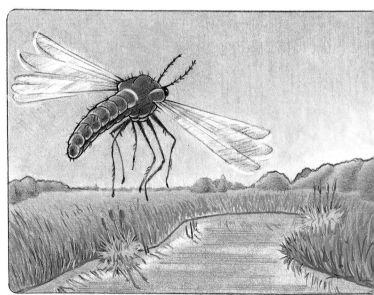

Mosquitoes lay hundreds of eggs in still pools of water. They are drawn to stagnant water by the smell of bacteria.

Mosquito, above and facing page

M O T h s

(Order: Lepidoptera)

Moths never grow old—they live only a couple of days! Their main purpose in the balance of nature is to serve as food for other, larger animals such as bats and birds. The most important activity for a moth during its brief life is to find a mate quickly and reproduce more moths. The male moth's nose plays a key role in this.

When the female moth emerges from her cocoon, she is odorless because she is not yet prepared to mate. But in just a few hours, she matures, ready to get down to the business of making more moths. At that time, she releases a fine mist of special perfume from two small pouches at the end of her abdomen. This perfume is very attractive to male moths. When just a few tiny molecules of the scent reach the male's antennae, he uses all of his energy to find the female. The female moth can attract males from as far away as three miles. During one scientific experiment, a male moth took just ten minutes to reach a scenting female one mile away. That's faster than a person can walk! Fortunately for male moths, most of them don't have to travel so far to find a mate.

The male moth's antennae, which look like tiny feathers or palm fronds, are much fancier than the female's. There are more than 40,000 sensory nerve cells on these feathery combs. With all of this smelling power, you'd think male moths would be bombarded by odors all the time. But the male moth's "nose" knows only one thing: the scent of the female's perfume.

Elephant hawk moth

A LITTLE DAB'LL DO

The female moth's perfume is incredibly strong. Only .01 microgram (a millionth of a gram) can, in theory, excite a billion or more males. And just how heavy is a gram? About the weight of a female moth.

There are tens of thousands of sensory nerve cells on the male moth's feathery antennae.

Clouded yellow moth, facing page

Ants

(Family: Formicidae)

What does an ant do if it finds a dead butterfly too heavy to carry back to the nest? It heads for home—lickety split—to get help. It pushes its stinger out of its abdomen and drags it along the ground as it crawls. At the same time, it presses on a scent gland that secretes a special chemical called a pheromone. By depositing traces of its pheromone, the ant makes a "sniffable" map for the members' colony to follow back to the prey.

An ant's scent map lasts only a couple of minutes, but other ants replenish the pheromone as they crawl along the same trail. Once the ants haul the food back to the nest, the scent trail vanishes—no more food, no more scent. Ants use scent and smell for other reasons, too. If an intruder disturbs the ants' nest, those ants first to notice emit a pheromone that says "Help! We're being attacked!" That's why if you disturb an ant hill, hundreds of ants will suddenly pour out of the holes and begin swarming around. If they're the kind that bite, you'd better scram!

Ants also secrete other pheromones to attract mates, to establish the order of dominance within the colony, and to identify members of the same colony. So while humans communicate with each other (mainly) through speech and gestures, ants "talk" by giving off scents and "listen" by smelling them.

Bulldog ant

SMELL? WHAT SMELL?

Each of the many ant species has its own unique set of pheromone scents that are top secret and not recognized by other species. For example, if a red ant crosses the pheromone trail a fire ant made, the red ant won't even notice! Its scent detectors are tuned in only to the pheromones of its own species.

Ants leave a trail of scent to lead other ants to a food source. In reality, this trail is invisible.

Ponerine ant, facing page

Bees

(Order: Hymenoptera)

Ouch! That hurts! When a bee stings you it discharges venom (poison) and an odor that may smell somewhat like a banana. This smell is a pheromone that serves as an alarm to other bees. If you are near the hive, the scent may provoke an angry mob of worker bees to swarm over you and sting you repeatedly. That's why most beekeepers are careful to wear protective clothing.

When a worker bee finds a new source of pollen, it releases a pheromone. As the scent of the pheromone wafts through the air, it attracts other worker bees. Soon, they show up at the flower to help collect the pollen.

How do bees detect these pheromones? Their antennae are covered with thousands of sense organs known as sensilla. Among them are tiny pits that contain olfactory (smelling) organs. Some of these olfactory pits react to many different odors, some only to special smells. The queen bee has up to 2,400 olfactory pits. Workers have about 1,600. The drones can have a whopping 37,800!

When a bee returns to the hive laden with nectar for making honey or with pollen to eat, it also carries the smell of the flower that produced the nectar or pollen. The worker bees in the hive use their sensilla to examine the smell clinging to the bee. Then, they set out to find the source of the nectar or the pollen by following traces of its smell in the air. They're helped in their search by a tail-wagging dance the returning bee performs for them—a "bee sign language" that shows the way to the source.

Honeybee

ONE BIG HAPPY FAMILY

Bees live together by the thousands in groups called colonies. A bee's home is called a hive. The bees who gather nectar to make honey are the female workers. Their stingless brothers are called drones. The mother of them all is called the queen.

A worker bee returns to its hive laden with pollen, leaving a scent trail for other workers to follow back to the source of the pollen.

Golden northern bumblebee, facing page

TURTles

(Order: Chelonia)

Turtles have been around a very long time. Fossils have been found of turtles that lived over 200 million years ago! Compare that with the amount of time humans in our current form have been around—only 40,000 years or so. But despite their lengthy stay on earth, turtles today are very similar to their prehistoric ancestors.

Turtles are toothless reptiles closely related to snakes and lizards. Most reptiles have well-developed nasal cavities (a space behind each nostril where the olfactory organs are), but turtles do not. Most reptiles evolved to depend a great deal on their sense of smell. But turtles appear to have survived over millions of years without even developing a sensitive nose! There is at least one exception, however. Snapping turtles apparently can find food in lakes even when the water is too dirty to see through. Scientists believe they do so by smelling their prey. The musk turtle has a gland that emits a very strong, unpleasant smell. This smell is so potent some people call these turtles "stinkpots." The smell may be an alarm that warns other turtles of danger. Or it may serve to attract a mate—after all, the turtles don't seem to mind the smell! It may even be the way musk turtles communicate with other musk turtles. Scientists don't know for certain.

Galapagos tortoise

TURTLE TROUBLE

Even though turtles are among the oldest species on the planet, many types are endangered. In some countries, people eat turtles. The green turtle is almost extinct because it has been hunted for its meat. Other people kill tortoises for their shells. Some rare species are dying out because their habitats (where they live) are destroyed by pollution or development. Some people are trying to save rare and endangered turtles by raising them in captivity or by preserving their natural habitats.

Unlike other reptiles, most turtles do not have a well-developed sense of smell.

Eastern box turtle, facing page

14

FROGS

(Order: Salientia)

There are over 2,000 species of frogs and toads. Toads look very similar to frogs but have rougher, drier skin and tend to spend more time on land than water-loving frogs. These amphibians (animals that live both in water and on land) live on every continent except the frozen land of Antarctica.

And just how well do frogs smell? From species to species, the frog's smelling ability differs a great deal. The leopard frog, for example, can be taught to distinguish between different smells. In one experiment, a frog was reluctant to eat food that had been dipped in rosewater, which has a strong floral smell. Frogs can also find their way back to their home pond—even frogs that are deaf and blind. They accomplish this primarily by using their sense of smell. However, the ability to orient themselves is also strong in frogs. (To orient yourself means to locate yourself in relation to something else—your home, for example.) If frogs are prevented from using their sense of smell (in scientific experiments, for example), they can still find their way home. You have many ways to orient yourself. Your home, your neighborhood, your school, your favorite park or playground—these are all landmarks to help you find your direction. The frog also uses many senses and signals to remember where it lives.

THE SMELL IS THE BELL

Tadpoles of certain amphibians swim around like an orderly school of small fish. They actually swim in rows. But if even a tiny amount of an "alarm" substance enters the water, order breaks down completely. The tadpoles head in every direction. Most swim towards the safety of deeper water. But if their sense of smell is blocked, tadpoles will continue to swim along as if nothing happened. The alarm bell is the smell!

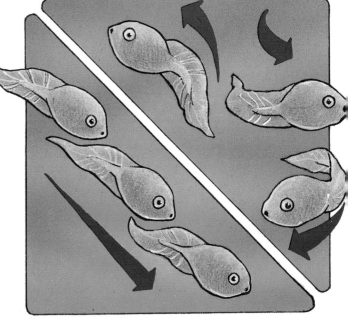

Tadpoles normally swim in orderly rows. If a smell that threatens them enters the water, they will scatter in all directions.

North American tree frog, facing page

Gerbils

(Genus: *Gerbillus*)

Just as ants, bees, and other insects communicate by smell, so does the Mongolian gerbil. This small rodent lives in eastern Mongolia, Northwest China, and western Manchuria. Today, it is also a common pet in America. It spends a great deal of its time rubbing its belly, chin, and neck over small objects.

Why does the gerbil behave in this interesting manner? To communicate with other gerbils. The gerbil has scent glands in the middle of its abdomen and on its chin and neck that secrete pheromones. To leave a mark or a trail of scent, the gerbil rubs its glands on twigs, stones, grass, or other objects in its small world. Scientists aren't completely sure what purpose the scent markings serve, but other gerbils are certainly interested in them. They can tell subtle differences in the odors of the scent trails and can identify where another gerbil has passed by.

There is an amazing feature of their fur that helps gerbils leave their scent trails. The hairs that cover the area near the scent glands have little grooves in them. This helps to move the scent along, as if it were being rolled down a tiny chute or pulled along with a straw.

ATTRACTION BY AROMA

All mammals produce scent, and some of it is used to attract a mate. We don't usually think of ourselves as having this in common with other animals, but consider the rituals we go through when we want to impress someone: we use minty toothpaste, splash on aftershave or dab on perfume, style our hair with mousse or gel, rub fragrant lotion on our skin, and wear freshly laundered clothes. All these things smell good and—we hope—make us attractive.

To leave a scent mark, the gerbil rubs a twig over the scent gland on its chin. Gerbils also have scent glands in their abdomen and on their neck.

Gerbil, above and facing page

BAts

(Order: Chiroptera)

Glossophagine bat

If we lost our sense of smell, we'd miss the smell of the earth after a rainstorm or cookies baking in the oven, but we'd survive just the same. If a fruit-eating bat lost its sense of smell, it would die. Unlike insect-eating bats that depend solely upon their sense of hearing to find food, fruit-eating bats rely on their keen sense of smell.

Bats may look like a cross between a rodent and a bird, but they are mammals, the only mammals that fly. The original reason mammals developed a sharp sense of smell was so they could feed at night and avoid becoming food for dinosaurs, which hunted during the day. Fruit-eating bats are relatives of those first mammals who began smelling their way to food in the dark because it was safer. The olfactory lobe—the area of the brain that processes smells—of a fruit bat is significantly larger than that of an insect-eating bat. Fruit bats feed at night and follow their nose to the tropical fruits they love: guavas, figs, bananas, and mangoes.

Fruit bats are strong fliers and sometimes travel long distances to feast at their favorite feeding areas. They have a hearty appetite and often will eat the equivalent of their own weight in fruit in a single evening.

There *is* one thing that can impair a bat's ability to smell its way to food: wind. On windy nights when smells are blown away, fruit-eating bats go hungry.

THE RIPE CHOICE

Fruit-eating bats are frugivores, meaning they eat only fruit. (Insectivores eat insects, herbivores eat plants, carnivores eat meat, and omnivores—like us—eat just about anything!) Even in the dark, without feeling the fruit, the frugivorous bat knows the difference between a ripe guava and one that is not yet ready to eat. By smell alone, the bat will select only the ripest fruit, leaving the unripe fruit to mature for a later meal.

Fruit-eating bats rely on their keen sense of smell to locate ripe tropical fruits.

Gothic bat, facing page

SNAKes

(Order: Squamata)

Green-headed racer

Many snakes find their prey by smelling the trail that the creature leaves behind it. This hunting technique is called trailing. Different kinds of snakes trail different kinds of food. The rat snake, for example, follows the scent of rodents, while the garter snake in your garden sniffs after insects. The American blind snake also tracks its favorite food, ants, by sense of smell. Humans taste many foods before deciding what we like best. But snakes know by instinct what prey suits them, as well as its distinct scent.

Trailing requires a keen sense of smell. Snakes have nostrils, the holes in the nose that let in air. But they also have a special organ on the roof of their mouth that aids them in smelling prey. This is called the Jacobson's organ. The snake uses this organ by flicking its tongue in and out of its mouth. When the tongue is out of the mouth, it picks up scent molecules hanging in the air. When it darts back in the mouth, it rubs these molecules onto the Jacobson's organ. From there, the sensory impulses are carried to the snake's brain, which interprets what the smell is and tells the snake what action to take. Snakes also flicker their tongues when they sense danger and are preparing to strike. If you come across a snake doing this, you should excuse yourself—fast!

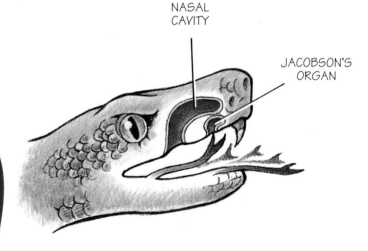

NASAL CAVITY

JACOBSON'S ORGAN

FEEL THE HEAT

Unlike many snakes, the rattlesnake does not trail its prey. It uses a heat-sensitive organ called a pit organ to hunt warm-blooded prey, whose warm bodies slightly change the temperature of the air around them. Pit organs are cavities in the snake's head, usually in front of and under the eyes. When the rattlesnake finds it prey (a mouse, for example), it bites it, injecting venom, and then lets it go. As the poisoned mouse tries to escape, the rattlesnake tracks its dying victim by following the warmth of the mouse's body, as well as the scent of its own venom.

When snakes flicker their tongues, they are actually bringing scent molecules from the air to the smelling organ on the roof of their mouth.

Black-tailed rattlesnake, facing page

Kiwis

(Apteryx australis)

New Zealand's kiwi may look like a feathered football with a soda straw nose, but in the world of birds it is a very special creature. About the size of a chicken, the kiwi has no tail, bad eyesight, and tiny little wings that won't even lift it off the ground.

But the kiwi has something no other bird has: the ability to smell worms *underground*. This is an important skill for a bird whose diet consists of earthworms and burrowing insects. By day these shy, shaggy birds hide in the forest underbrush. At night they leave their hiding places and become mighty earthworm hunters, poking and probing the forest floor for the juicy worms they love.

Other birds have nostrils close to their heads and locate their prey by seeing or feeling it. Birds such as starlings or waders feed by probing for buried insects, just as the kiwi does. But these other birds find their food by digging a hole in the ground and peering down their bills for their hidden meal. The kiwi alone can smell insects underground.

Unlike every other bird's, the kiwi's nostrils are at the tip of its bill. How do kiwis snuffle in the soil without getting a snoutful of dirt? No one knows for sure, but the hair-like feathers at the base of its bill probably help. Like whiskers on mammals, they may keep the kiwi out of too-tight spots. Or, like our nose hairs, they may filter out dirt particles as the kiwi sniffs around in the earth.

MIND YOUR OWN BEESWAX

Besides the kiwi, the only other insect-eating bird known to rely heavily on its sense of smell is the African honey guide. A Portuguese missionary in East Africa discovered this when he lit some beeswax candles. The unlit candles attracted no birds. But when the priest lit the candles, the church was soon filled with the small birds. (Why? Because smells are intensified by heat.) The honey guides flew right up to the candles—and *ate* the warm wax!

Kiwis dine on burrowing insects and earthworms. They are the only birds able to smell insects underground.

Brown kiwi, above and facing page

Prairie Dogs

(Genus: *Cynomys*)

Prairie dogs, so-named for their bark-like call, are among the most sociable of creatures. These rodents live in large colonies, and their social structure is organized around the sense of smell. A prairie dog town may have as many as thirty districts, and each district houses a clan of about forty members. The walls of a prairie dog town are invisible to the human eye, but not to the prairie dog nose. These walls are all scent boundaries that mark borders.

It is important for an individual prairie dog to be good at smelling these boundaries, because it is strictly forbidden to cross over into unfamiliar territory. In fact, if a prairie dog does cross a scent boundary, whether on purpose or by mistake, the unlucky animal will immediately be attacked by the whole family of invaded prairie dogs. These scent boundaries give off a definite message: visitors are not welcome.

Sometimes a prairie dog gets the urge to ignore these invisible "No Trespassing" signs. Most often, it is the bold young males who want to explore unfamiliar territory. But the adventurous youth doesn't just use force. He may actually try to make friends first, so he'll have some allies in the new neighborhood. He does this by flirting with the females. If all goes well and he is allowed into the new camp, some of these females may become his mates.

Whitetail prairie dog

BORDER PATROL

Female prairie dogs also patrol scent boundaries. If a female trespasses, a resident may cautiously approach her and show her teeth. In effect, she is asking the stranger to show her "passport." The visitor may raise her tail, showing her scent glands. But the wrong scent can set off a battle, with both prairie dogs biting and running. The fight will end when both pick up the scent of the boundary line and retreat to their own side.

Prairie dogs mark their territory with scent boundaries. If a prairie dog from another neighborhood tries to cross this invisible border, a resident will most likely threaten or attack the intruder.

Black-tailed prairie dog, facing page

Cats

(Family: Felidae)

A cat's petite nose is actually the smallest part of its keen olfactory system. Behind its nose is a maze of bone and cavities that contains a lining with 200 million olfactory cells. As the cat breathes, air is warmed, moistened, and passed across this lining and over the olfactory cells. Signals are then sent to the olfactory lobe of the cat's brain, which interprets the smells.

Cats have a reputation for being finicky about their food. But it is actually the smell of meat, rather than the taste, that cats react to. A cat who doesn't like liver, for example, really doesn't like the *smell* of liver and will refuse to eat it. In fact, if a cat has a cold and can't smell, it won't eat because it can't be sure its food is actually food.

Cats, like dogs, have two openings in the roof of the mouth lined with olfactory cells. This is called the vomeronasal organ, and it is very similar to the snake's Jacobson's organ. You've probably seen a cat stretch its neck, open its mouth, and curl its lips in a funny smile. What it's doing is bringing air to the vomeronasal organ for a good whiff, just as snakes flicker their tongue to rub scent molecules on their Jacobson's organ. Cats mostly use their sense of smell to locate and investigate stationary objects, such as their food dish or an intoxicating ball of catnip.

Ocelot

HEADS OR TAILS

Cats have glands in various parts of their bodies that secrete pheromones. These leave scent messages for other animals about the cat's territory and its catty activities. One area with scent glands is the forehead. When your cat rubs its head against your legs or against the living room couch, it is marking its territory and making it familiar with its own smell. Cats use smell as a form of greeting, first going nose to nose and then turning around and lifting their tails. Your cat may do this to you, too—probably not the best way to say "how do you do?" in a human social setting, but it's very good manners in the cat world.

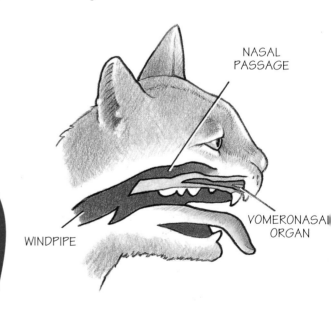

NASAL PASSAGE

VOMERONASAL ORGAN

WINDPIPE

Cats have two openings in the roof of the mouth lined with olfactory cells. This is called the vomeronasal organ, and it is very similar to the snake's Jacobson's organ.

Asian lion, facing page

S a L m on

(Genera: *Salmo* and *Oncorhynchus*)

Salmon go far with their noses—really far. Without a map or a compass, a salmon will travel as many as 1,000 miles from the ocean back to the river of its birth, using only its nose for navigation.

A salmon's sense of smell is very sensitive, picking up even the faintest of odors. The fish's nose is made up of two separate openings, called olfactory pits, connected by a pair of U-shaped tubes. Water flows in through the first opening while the salmon swims and breathes, then flows out through the second opening. Odors in the water stimulate the olfactory receptors—cells that receive smells—which send information to the salmon's brain. A salmon's nose is not connected to its throat and mouth, like ours is. Instead, it is attached to an area of its brain that evaluates the smells in water.

Shortly after a salmon hatches in the freshwater of a mountain stream, it swims down into the ocean. As many as seven years later, it begins the long trip home. For two to three weeks, it swims day and night without eating or sleeping. Moving along at $2\frac{1}{2}$ to $4\frac{1}{2}$ miles per hour, the fish swims hundreds of miles through the ocean and up a series of rivers to the exact river it was born in. Once salmon reach their home waters, they lay and fertilize their eggs, and then die. This dramatic rite of nature is called the spawning of salmon.

Salmo fontinalis

LED BY THE NOSE

Salmon are drawn homeward by the smell of their home waters and the smell of young salmon in the river or stream where they were born. Their keen sense of smell also alerts them to trouble. The skin of an injured fish gives off a scent that warns other fish of danger.

Swimming upriver against the current, salmon sometimes have to launch themselves into the air to climb waterfalls.

Red salmon, facing page

Lemurs

(Family: Lemuridae)

Ring-tailed lemur

The lemur is a small monkey-like creature that, along with humans, is a primate. Lemurs live on the island of Madagascar, off the east coast of Africa. The ring-tailed lemur has a most impressive tail, striped like a raccoon's and bushy as a squirrel's. Lemurs are among the most ancient of animals. They swing from the trees at all levels of the forest.

The lemur has a well-developed olfactory center in its brain. Like the skunk, the lemur has musk glands that secrete a very foul odor. The main purpose of the lemur's odor is to communicate with other lemurs.

The male lemur has musk glands on its tail and forearms. To mark its territory, the lemur rubs its strong scent on twigs and anything else it happens to pass on its forest rounds. When a male prepares to do battle with other males during the mating season, he drags his tail across his musk glands over and over again, covering the tail with scent. The tail then becomes his not-so-secret weapon as he waves it in the breeze to ward off other males. The lemur's waving black-and-white ringed tail is first a visual warning signal. When it is permeated with scent, it becomes a definite "Do Not Enter" sign. Because their tails are so important to them, lemurs comb them often with a special grooming claw on the second digit (toe) of each foot.

SCENT STAND

Why do lemurs stand on their head? These animals do headstands to press their rear ends against a tree trunk. In a zoo, they will do it against the wall of a cage. This is another way of marking territory with scent. The gray gentle lemur is similar to the ring-tailed lemur. Its upper arms have glands that secrete a liquid that is milky-white and smells like beeswax. Not only lemurs can smell this; humans too can pick up the scent from neighboring tree trunks.

During the mating season, male lemurs cover their tails with a foul scent from their musk glands and wave them in the breeze to ward off other males.

Collared lemur, facing page

Salamanders

(Order: Caudata)

A salamander may look like a lizard, but it is not. It lacks both the claws and scales that characterize lizards. Like the frog, the salamander is an amphibian, an animal that lives both in water and on land. Salamanders depend upon their noses to find a good meal, such as a small worm or some shellfish

The Texas blind salamander, creeping around in dark caves, searches for its food by using its sense of smell. In the Ozark mountains of Arkansas lives the Grotto salamander. (A grotto is a cave, this salamander's natural habitat.) Like its cousin in Texas, it too sniffs out its food and has little use for good vision. In fact, skin grows over their eyes as salamanders mature. Most salamanders have nostrils and nasal cavities similar to humans'. The animal inhales airborne odors, and olfactory receptors in the nasal cavity detect them.

But other types of salamanders don't have such conventional noses. They don't even have lungs. They breathe and smell through their skin! Oxygen passes directly through their moist, flexible, thin skin.

Salamanders use their sense of smell for more than food. During the mating season, male and female salamanders smell for each other. They have special glands that become active during the mating season. Different types of salamanders have these glands on different parts of their bodies. Some have them on the head and chin, others on the tail, and still others on the abdomen.

Red-spotted newt

MATING MATCH

During the mating season, salamanders behave rather oddly. A male and female face each other. They tap each other on the nose. Then they touch each other on the chin. They look like they're throwing a few good punches in a salamander boxing match! They do this only during the mating season, after their glands start to secrete. This strange ritual allows the salamanders to check each other out before mating.

Some species of salamander breathe and smell through their thin, flexible skin.

Long-tailed salamander, facing page

DOGs

(Canis familiaris)

Bernese mountain dog

When a dog twitches and barks in its sleep, we sometimes say it's dreaming about chasing rabbits. But dogs don't dream about the rabbits themselves, they dream about their smell. Dogs "see" the world with their noses. In fact, the largest part of a dog's brain is devoted to interpreting smells.

Dogs' long snouts have 10 to 15 times more area for sensory cells than our noses do. The inside of a dog's nose is lined with up to 200 million olfactory receptor cells. Like cats, dogs also smell through two small openings on the roof of their mouth, called the vomeronasal organ.

You can act tough in front of a growling dog, but it will probably know you're scared anyway. This is because dogs can smell moods. Strong emotions produce chemical reactions in our bodies. Humans usually can't detect these subtle scents, but dogs aren't fooled.

Dogs "talk" to each other by leaving scent messages behind for other dogs to "read." Pockets between the pads of their paws leave a scent trail on the ground that can last for days. And you've probably seen the neighborhood dog relieving itself on every bush on the street. This is its way of marking territory. A dog's urine reveals its age, whether it's male or female, whether it's the poodle next door or the spaniel across the tracks, and whether it was excited, frightened, or hostile when it passed by. The ground around your neighborhood is your dog's newspaper, providing it with all the information it needs to know about what's going on in its world.

P.S. Just as no two people have identical fingerprints, each dog has a unique nose print.

HOT ON THE TRAIL

Their powerful sense of smell and willingness to serve makes dogs very good workers, as well as wonderful companions. German shepherds and other breeds help police by sniffing out illegal substances or tracking criminals on the run. Other dogs work with rescue teams to find lost or injured people.

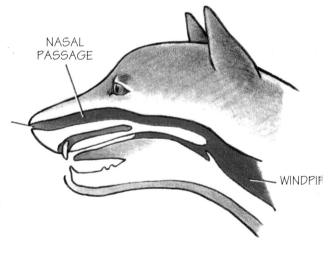

NASAL PASSAGE

NOSTRIL

WINDPIPE

Dogs have 10 to 15 times more smelling area inside their noses than humans do.

Shar pei, facing page

Turkey Vultures

(Cathartes aura)

With their bare, red heads, dark feathers, and hunched posture, turkey vultures aren't very pretty to look at. But these birds have keen eyes and can see their prey from great distances. It is their powerful sense of smell, however, that sets them apart from other birds.

These large birds, found from southern Canada to South America, are scavengers, which means they eat dead animals. It's a dirty job, but somebody's got to do it, and turkey vultures seem content to serve as the sanitation workers of the animal kindgom. Although they do take live prey if it is available, turkey vultures most often dine on dead animals (called carrion) and garbage. By eating carrion, vultures perform the useful service of disposing of decaying material that might otherwise be a breeding ground for dangerous bacteria.

Believe it or not, turkey vultures have been known to lend a helping hand—or rather, nose—to people. These birds gather around areas where underground fuel pipes have fractured, attracted by the chemical used to give natural gas an odor. The turkey vulture's powerful sense of smell can lead engineers to a gas leak much more quickly than their own laborious search would.

Turkey vultures, also called buzzards, are powerful, graceful fliers. They spend much of their time soaring high in the air, looking for food. As they fly over the land, odors given off by a dead animal alert the turkey vulture that a meal might be nearby. The vulture circles in the air, drawn closer and closer by the smell of decaying carrion.

A REAL STEAL

Turkey vultures are well-liked by other members of the vulture family, but not for their wonderful personalities. The turkey vulture's cousins—the North American black vulture, the American condor, and the California condor—can't smell worth a hoot, so they rely on the turkey vulture's keen sense of smell to help them find food. The cousins watch the turkey vulture's hunting flights, using the bird as a scout. Once it finds food, the cousin vultures descend on the bird and steal its meal.

The turkey vulture circles in the air over the carrion on which it feeds. It is drawn closer and closer by the smell of decaying flesh.

Turkey vulture, above and facing page

Sharks

Sand tiger shark

Imagine not using your nose to breathe, but only to find food. That's what a shark does. Sharks are carnivores (meat-eaters) and hunt their prey, mostly other fish, by scent. This is called chemosensing, detecting chemical reactions with sensory organs. A blindfolded shark can locate dead crabs in less than a minute. Because it depends on smell for survival, the olfactory lobes in a shark's brain are very large. By contrast, the optic lobes, which process sight, are small because vision is not very important to the shark.

Sharks often hunt injured prey. They can smell a single drop of blood in 25 gallons of water—about the amount it would take to fill a small wading pool—and an injured fish will bleed a lot more than a drop. Sharks also pursue healthy, active fish, especially if the fish are agitated and give off a stronger than usual scent. A shark can follow an odor trail very precisely, tracking exactly the path of a fish swimming ahead, out of sight. Sharks have been known to attack humans, particularly injured swimmers or divers. Even a small amount of blood in the water can attract a shark from a considerable distance—unless it's shark blood, that is. The smell of injured shark triggers an alarm reaction in other sharks and they stay away.

Sharks are often called the "hounds of the sea" because their noses are as sensitive as a dog's. Another of their nicknames is the "swimming nose."

MAN-EATING SHARKS

Terrifying movies have been made about sharks attacking bathers at the beach, but such attacks seldom happen. Generally, sharks stay out of the shallow water where people are most likely to go swimming. As more people venture into deeper waters with scuba equipment, shark attacks are becoming more common.

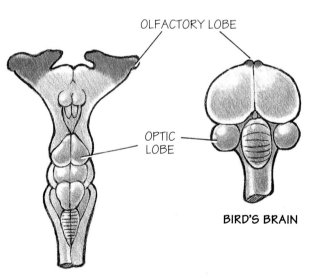

OLFACTORY LOBE

OPTIC LOBE

BIRD'S BRAIN

SHARK'S BRAIN

The olfactory lobes in a shark's brain are very large compared to the optic lobe, which handles sight. By contrast, the olfactory lobes in a bird's brain are just two little nubs.

Great white shark, facing page

ELEPHANTS

(Elephas maximus or Loxodonta africana)

The elephant has the biggest nose in the world, and no wonder: it is the largest land mammal of all. Elephants have a very keen sense of smell, which is a good thing since they do not see very well. They use their sense of smell to locate food, find mates, and detect enemies. When a herd of wild elephants is out walking together they may pause suddenly, their trunks swaying, and then lift them to sniff the air all together.

An elephant's sense of smell is so sensitive it can detect the scent of a human being three miles away. Unfortunately, their sense of smell is no protection against big game hunters and ivory collectors, who have hunted these intelligent creatures so heavily they are now endangered species.

Elephants are very sociable creatures, and they use their sense of smell to keep track of their family members. Elephants leave something for each other to smell; they have glands on their faces that release scents used for marking territory and for attracting a mate. When an elephant smells the ground or trees, it is figuring out which of its neighbors or family members has passed by.

The elephant's nose is far more than just an organ of smell. Asian elephants are so dexterous with their trunk, they can pick up an object as tiny as a coin. Elephants are very affectionate and loyal, but they lack arms for hugging. This doesn't stop them: elephant parents hug their children with their trunks.

Asiatic elephant

TRUNK PRACTICE

A baby elephant, called a calf, does not have the use of its trunk. The trunk just hangs from the calf's head, floppy and useless. Like a human child, it must learn coordination. The first thing the calf discovers about its trunk is that it can suck on the tip of it, just as human infants suck their thumbs. After about three months, the young elephant begins to learn all the varied uses of this invaluable organ.

Elephants hold their trunks high like flags when they sniff the air.

African elephant, facing page

HUMANS

(Homo sapiens)

Some fresh bread has just popped out of the oven, still piping hot. You know this even though you're in the other room. How? Tiny particles of the chemical that make up the smell of the bread float in the air. There are more particles in the kitchen than in the room you're in. For this reason, the smell of the bread is stronger in the kitchen, closer to the source of the smell.

The particles enter your nostrils. Each nostril leads into a nasal passage, which in turn opens into a nasal cavity. You breathe air, with all of its chemical particles, into the nasal cavities. There, particles swirl around and stimulate the olfactory membrane, which rests on the roof of the cavity. It is only about the size of a dime and contains about 600,000 olfactory receptors. A similar membrane inside a dog's nose is 10 to 15 times larger and contains about 2 million olfactory cells!

Mucous cells keep the lining of the nasal passage moist. This is very important for smelling because chemical particles must dissolve in order to be smelled. The dissolved particles come in contact with nerve endings that look like little hairs. They connect directly to the olfactory lobe, the part of the brain that interprets smell.

Compared with many other animals, our sense of smell is poor. In humans, vision dominates all the other senses. Even so, most people can tell the differences between thousands of smells. And we can learn more smells than sounds, even though hearing is more important than smell for getting along in the world.

SCENTS AND SENSIBILITY

Humans use fragrance to attract one another. Some women wear perfume, and some men use cologne or after-shave. Some people do not like the natural smell of humans. Micro-organisms called bacteria act on people's sweat. The result is body odor. To prevent body odor, people use products to hide the odor (deodorants) and to limit sweating (anti-perspirants). Humans also secrete scents that communicate fear, hostility, excitement, and other strong emotions. But most people have lost the ability to detect these subtle smells, and the many scented products we use mask them anyway.

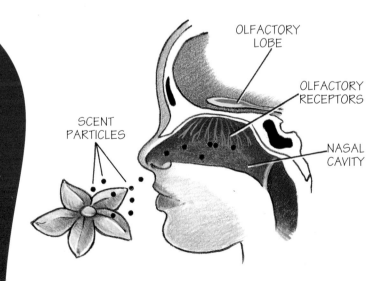

As we inhale, scent particles are drawn into the nasal cavity, where olfactory nerves turn them into signals to be sent to the brain.

44

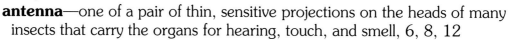

GLOSSARIZED INDEX

This glossarized index will help you find specific information about the sense of smell. It will also help you understand the meaning of some of the words used in this book.

olfactory—related to the sense of smell

olfactory lobe—the part of the brain that interprets smells, 5, 20, 28, 40

olfactory receptor—a cell that receives smells, 5, 28, 30, 34, 36, 44

order—fourth-largest category of **taxonomy**

pheromone—a substance secreted by an animal that influences the behavior of other animals of the same species. Pheromones are perceived by the sense of smell, 5, 10, 12, 18, 28, 32

pit organ—a cavity on the heads of some snakes that senses heat given off by warm-blooded prey; usually, pit organs are located under and in front of the snake's eyes, 22

prairie dogs, 26

proboscis—a long snout or trunk, such as the elephant has, or a thin beaklike tube, such as the mosquito has

salamander, 34

salmon, 30

sensilla—plural of sensillum, a hair-like sense organ consisting of one cell or a few cells; mosquitoes and other insects have sensilla on their **antennae**, 8, 12

sharks, 40

snakes, 22

spawning—to deposit eggs; after salmon spawn, they die, 30

species—narrowest category of **taxonomy**; members of a species look similar and can reproduce with each other

taxonomy—scientific system of classification for all living things; the seven taxonomic categories, from broadest to narrowest, are kindgom, phylum, class, order, family, genus, species

toads, 16

turkey vultures, 38

turtles, 14

vomeronasal organ—smelling organ on the roof of the mouths of dogs and cats, similar to the **Jacobson's organ**, 28, 36

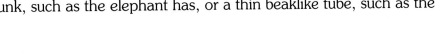

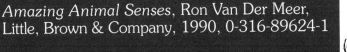

Other books about animals and the five senses:

Amazing Animal Senses, Ron Van Der Meer, Little, Brown & Company, 1990, 0-316-89624-1

Animal Senses, Jim Flegg, Newington Press, 1991, 1-878137-21-2

Extraordinary Eyes: How Animals See the World, Sandra Sinclair, R.R. Bowker, 1991, 0-8037-0806-8

Fingers & Feelers, Henry Pluckrose, Watts, Franklin, Incorporated, 1990, 0-531-14050-4

Tongues & Tasters, Henry Pluckrose, Watts, Franklin, Incorporated, 1990, 0-531-14049-0

Touch, Taste & Smell, Steve Parker, Watts, Franklin, Incorporated, 1989, 0-531-10655-1

Why Do Cats' Eyes Glow in the Dark?: (And Other Questions Kids Ask about Animals), Joanne Settel & Nancy Baggett, Atheneum-MacMillan, 1988, 0-689-31267-9

Photo credits:

pg. 3:
(boxer) Animals Animals © Ralph A. Reinhold
(honeybee) Animals Animals © Stephen Dalton

pg. 6:
Animals Animals © D. R. Specker

pg. 7:
Animals Animals © J. A. L. Cooke

pg. 8:
Animals Animals © Stephen Dalton

pg. 9:
Animals Animals © Stephen Dalton

pg. 10:
Animals Animals © Kathie Atkinson/Oxford Scientific Films

pg. 11:
Animals Animals © Michael Fogden

pg. 12:
Animals Animals © Stephen Dalton

pg. 13:
Animals Animals © Robert A. Lubeck

pg. 14:
Animals Animals © Joe McDonald

pg. 15:
Animals Animals © Zig Leszczynski

pg. 16:
Animals Animals © Zig Leszczynski

pg. 17:
Animals Animals © Alastair Shay/Oxford Scientific Films

pg. 18:
Animals Animals © Zig Leszczynski

pg. 19:
Animals Animals © Richard Kolar

pg. 20:
Animals Animals © Oxford Scientific Films

pg. 21:
Animals Animals © Michael Fogden

pg. 22:
Animals Animals © Michael Fogden

pg. 23:
Animals Animals © Joe McDonald

pg. 24:
Photo Researchers, Inc. © Tom McHugh

pg. 25:
Photo Researchers, Inc. © Tom McHugh

pg. 26:
Animals Animals © Don Enger

pg. 27:
Animals Animals © Richard Kolar

pg. 28:
Animals Animals © John Chellman

pg. 29:
Animals Animals © John Chellman

pg. 30:
Animals Animals © Robert Maier

pg. 31:
Animals Animals © Johnny Johnson

pg. 32:
Animals Animals © Frank Roberts

pg. 33:
Animals Animals © Mark Pidgeon/Oxford Scientific Films

pg. 34:
Animals Animals © Bates Littlehales

pg. 35:
Animals Animals © Zig Leszczynski

pg. 36:
Animals Animals © Gérard Lacz

pg. 37:
Animals Animals © Robert Pearcy

pg. 38:
Animals Animals © C. W. Schwartz

pg. 39:
Animals Animals © Joe McDonald

pg. 40:
Animals Animals © C. C. Lockwood

pg. 41:
Animals Animals © James Watt

pg. 42:
Animals Animals © M. Austerman

pg. 43:
Animals Animals © Terry G. Murphy

pg. 44:
Animals Animals © C. C. Lockwood

pg. 45:
Earth Scenes © Jerry Cooke

BIZARRE & BEAUTIFUL SERIES

A spirited and fun investigation of the mysteries of the five senses in the animal kingdom.

Each title is 8¹/₂″ x 11″, 48 pages, $14.95 hardcover, with color photographs and illustrations throughout.

Bizarre & Beautiful Ears (available 9/93)
Bizarre & Beautiful Eyes (available 9/93)
Bizarre & Beautiful Feelers (available 10/93)
Bizarre & Beautiful Noses (available 9/93)
Bizarre & Beautiful Tongues (available 11/93)

RAINBOW WARRIOR ARTISTS SERIES

W hat is a Rainbow Warrior Artist? It is a person who strives to live in harmony with the Earth and all living creatures, and who tries to better the world while living his or her life in a creative way.

Each title is written by Reavis Moore with a foreword by LeVar Burton, and is 8¹/₂″ x 11″, 48 pages, $14.95 hardcover, with color photographs and illustrations.

Native Artists of Africa (available 1/94)
Native Artists of North America

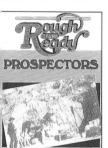

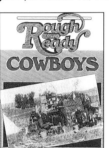

ROUGH AND READY SERIES

L earn about the men and women who settled the American frontier. Explore the myths and legends about these coura-geous individuals and learn about the environmental, cultural, and economic legacies they left to us.

Each title is written by A. S. Gintzler and is 48 pages, 8¹/₂″ x 11″, $12.95 hardcover, with two-color illustrations and duotone archival photographs.

Rough and Ready Cowboys (available 4/94)
Rough and Ready Homesteaders (available 4/94)
Rough and Ready Prospectors (available 4/94)

AMERICAN ORIGINS SERIES

M any of us are the third and fourth generation of our families to live in America. Learn what our great-great grandparents experienced when they arrived here and how much of our lives are still intertwined with theirs.

Each title is 48 pages, 8¹/₂″ x 11″, $12.95 hardcover, with two-color illustrations and duotone archival photographs.

Tracing Our German Roots, Leda Silver (available 12/93)
Tracing Our Irish Roots, Sharon Moscinski (available 10/93)
Tracing Our Italian Roots, Kathleen Lee (available 10/93)
Tracing Our Jewish Roots, Miriam Sagan (available 12/93)

EXTREMELY WEIRD SERIES

All of the titles are written by Sarah Lovett, 8¹/2" x 11", 48 pages, $9.95 paperbacks, with color photographs and illustrations.

Extremely Weird Bats
Extremely Weird Birds
Extremely Weird Endangered Species
Extremely Weird Fishes
Extremely Weird Frogs
Extremely Weird Insects
Extremely Weird Mammals (available 8/93)
Extremely Weird Micro Monsters (available 8/93)
Extremely Weird Primates
Extremely Weird Reptiles
Extremely Weird Sea Creatures
Extremely Weird Snakes (available 8/93)
Extremely Weird Spiders

X-RAY VISION SERIES

Each title in the series is 8¹/2" x 11", 48 pages, $9.95 paperback, with color photographs and illustrations and written by Ron Schultz.

Looking Inside the Brain
Looking Inside Cartoon Animation
Looking Inside Caves and Caverns
 (available 11/93)
Looking Inside Sports Aerodynamics
Looking Inside Sunken Treasure
Looking Inside Telescopes and the Night Sky

THE KIDDING AROUND TRAVEL GUIDES

All of the titles listed below are 64 pages and $9.95 paperbacks, except for Kidding Around the National Parks and Kidding Around Spain, which are 108 pages and $12.95 paperbacks.

Kidding Around Atlanta
Kidding Around Boston, 2nd ed.
Kidding Around Chicago, 2nd ed.
Kidding Around the Hawaiian Islands
Kidding Around London
Kidding Around Los Angeles
Kidding Around the National Parks
 of the Southwest
Kidding Around New York City, 2nd ed.
Kidding Around Paris
Kidding Around Philadelphia
Kidding Around San Diego
Kidding Around San Francisco
Kidding Around Santa Fe
Kidding Around Seattle
Kidding Around Spain
Kidding Around Washington, D.C., 2nd ed.

MASTERS OF MOTION SERIES

Each title in the series is 10¹/4" x 9", 48 pages, $9.95 paperback, with color photographs and illustrations.

How to Drive an Indy Race Car
 David Rubel
How to Fly a 747
 Tim Paulson
How to Fly the Space Shuttle
 Russell Shorto

THE KIDS EXPLORE AMERICA SERIES

Each title is written by kids for kids by the Westridge Young Writers Workshop, 7" x 9", with photographs and illustrations by the kids.

Kids Explore America's Hispanic Heritage
112 pages, $7.95 paper
Kids Explore America's African-American Heritage
128 pages, $8.95 paper
Kids Explore the Gifts of Children with Special Needs
112 pages, $8.95 paper (available 2/94)
Kids Explore America's Japanese Heritage
112 pages, $8.95 paper (available 4/94)

ENVIRONMENTAL TITLES

Habitats: Where the Wild Things Live
Randi Hacker and Jackie Kaufman
8¹/2" x 11", 48 pages, color illustrations, $9.95 paper

The Indian Way: Learning to Communicate with Mother Earth
Gary McLain
7" x 9", 114 pages, illustrations, $9.95 paper

Rads, Ergs, and Cheeseburgers: The Kids' Guide to Energy and the Environment
Bill Yanda
7" x 9", 108 pages, two-color illustrations, $13.95 paper

The Kids' Environment Book: What's Awry and Why
Anne Pedersen
7" x 9", 192 pages, two-color illustrations, $13.95 paper